MARY GR

Rental diaries

Thoughts from
my four walls in Florence

The Florentine / Press

Rental diaries

MARY GRAY

ISBN 978-88-97696-21-6

First edition: June 2020

2020 B'Gruppo srl, Prato

Imprint | *Collana*: The Florentine Press

www.theflorentinepress.com

layout and cover illustration: Leo Cardini | flod.it

Table of contents

5 *Introduction*

9 A charming ground floor...store
11 An unexpected welcome
13 Fuseboxes and forgiveness
17 Significant others
19 Safe words
21 UFOs
25 Hidden awful things
27 Takeover tenants
29 Our sinks, our selves
31 Neighborhood loyalties
33 Tutto incluso
35 Business ideas
39 Things that bug me
41 La privacy
43 What-ifs
47 Concessions
49 The blondes upstairs
51 Handymen
53 Serious
57 Comebacks
59 The palazzo philharmonic
61 Rear Window experiences
63 Tidying up
67 Training
69 Collecting
71 Sitcoms
75 Running gags
77 Couched in
81 Balance
83 Beat

INTRODUCTION

This collection is being launched as my recurring Rental Diaries column reaches its 30th edition. Yay! A few months ago, I also reached my 30th year. Or, wait, finished my 30th year. To simplify: I turned 30.

It's fine, I know, I'm fine. I'm a whole lot of everything, actually—excited and zesty and melancholic and curious about all that's to come. I've never adhered to an arbitrary list of "shoulds" to accomplish in a certain timeframe. Still, I can't pretend that the birthday didn't prompt some reflection. Milestones have a way of doing that, *sempre*.

My dear mother came to visit me a few days after I turned the page, and it was like soul balm to see my life through her eyes. Because really, who among us doesn't want to make her parents proud, and doesn't also wonder if she ever properly can? We were slurping up *pici all'aglione* at Del Fagioli when she asked me *that* question. The one about whether I "plan to stay" in Florence or what—if it felt like home, or if my current world as a Tuscan tumbleweed precluded any sense of permanence. I'm not sure what I said in reply, or if I'll ever have total certainty about what home means to me. I do know that in that moment, home felt a lot like sharing a hot plate of *pici* in Florence with my mother.

Rental Diaries came about three years ago, after I spent five-ish months hunting for an affordable one-bedroom home to rent, one in no immediate danger of becoming an Airbnb. Finding one of those is quite a feat, as all residents here are aware. I'd planned to focus on the highs and lows of the search itself, mixing in stories from friends and colleagues to keep people on their toes. You'll see that in the early, short, slice-of-life columns.

But Rental Diaries really came about when I stopped trying to make anybody proud, least of all myself, and just tried to tell the truth and have a laugh about it all. I'd grown a little tired of reading flowery, *Chicken Soup*-style manifestos about the healing powers of the *dolce vita*, tales of reformed corporate hustlers tamed by hearing Duomo bells and tasting food for the first time. Yet the other side, those ubiquitous, Facebook-ready rants about Italy's inefficiency, unfair tax laws, and unforgiving patriarchy didn't quite capture my reality, either. As with most things, so many shades of grey seemed unaddressed, so much nuance and humor and humility lacking. *Pietra serena* is never the full story, is it?

The Rental Diaries aren't the full story, either. Not mine, not yours, certainly not Florence's. My scattered notebooks and email drafts—those very official modes of writerly storage—are littered with characters, vignettes, and half-formed threads still waiting to take flight. How is it that in thirty columns, I've not once name-checked Stefano, my ex-landlord's endearing assistant, who was never *not* wheezing like he'd just run a marathon when he came to collect the rent? Or how, when my roommates and I couldn't be home for the handoff, we'd hide the cash for him inside *Infinite Jest,* since it wasn't like anyone was ever going to get around to reading it? Why haven't I told you about the couple two floors above me now, who wriggled my housekey out of the lock when it snapped in two one time, or about my northern Italian neighbors who barely nod in my direction, yet quietly rallied the whole building to petition my landlady to let me keep my dog?

I've had a lot of time to comb through these and other memories during Covid-19 lockdown. They all feel like home, and like a soft place to land when my four rented walls started to close in on me amid this craziness. Plus, yesterday I got a surprise text message from my mom, letting me know that she and my dad just bought a house for their next phase. It looks like home, too. I just double-checked the photo and it turns out the bricks are white. Somehow I'd been picturing them as grey.

Con affetto, in affitto,

Mary Gray

Florence, June 2020

Being pursued as a potential tenant was highly unusual and more satisfying than it should have been.

Vol. 1

A charming ground floor...store

Pre-visit, the contract seemed to be exactly what I was looking for—the owners were searching for a reliable long-term resident to look after their renovated one-bedroom in San Frediano. Post-visit, the agency called me during work hours, a litmus test for my interest level.

Being pursued as a potential tenant was highly unusual and more satisfying than it should have been.

"It's not going to work," I said smugly. (Renaissance city real estate agents were bringing out a side of me I hardly knew existed, and I was loving it.) "For me it's *fondamentale* that taking up residence is a possibility, but I can't do that here, since the owners have illegally converted a ground-floor store into an apartment." It felt good to call out business BS for once. #NastyWoman!1!!

The agent played dumb at first, calling out to a colleague who may or may not have actually been present in her office. "*Ma*, Lorenzo*, is it true that you can't take up residence in that via Pisana bilocale?" Her mouth pointed back at the phone, she mumbled something fatalistic about how I'd have a hard time finding anything nicer *in centro*. At least *these* honest owners, she urged, were willing to give out a *stable* contract—that is, a 6+6 year agreement, the type used for commercial leases, and grounds for immediate dismissal if the police ever show up.

At this point I just needed to get off the phone, so I pulled the "it's out of my budget anyway" card.

"*Ah, ecco. Now* you tell me the truth!" the agent said knowingly.

**Name changed*

Vol. 2

An unexpected welcome

Sam is the son of a teacher and a writer—professions that people who land in Florence often have or hope for. His family's was supposed to be a short sabbatical from their suburban life, but ended up being a two-year stay during Sam's teenage years.

He recalls, vividly, the night they arrived jetlagged, listless expressions all around and luggage not necessarily so. A leg of their trip had been delayed, but rather than reschedule the apartment visit they'd set for that evening, his parents decided to tough it out and show up an hour late. All in the name of adjusting.

The Florentine owner had been very agreeable with the kind Massachusetts family, but the visit, Sam says, felt alarmingly hurried, so much so that even a 16-year-old could pick up on it. Something about the way this guy was herding his parents around the place felt...off. What was he hiding? Why wasn't there time to go upstairs, exactly?

Sam's mother opened her mouth to ask a question, but thought better of it and said, "You seem to be in a rush, we're sorry, we'll get out of your way."

The owner let out a huge sigh of relief. "I'm sorry. This was a bad idea. But the truth is it's my birthday and I'm late for the party."

"Aaah!" his mother exclaimed, smiling and eager to please the accommodating *proprietario*. *"Buon natale*!"

And with that, they were out the door.

Vol. 3

Fuseboxes and forgiveness

The Lady Downstairs is not a washed-up horror film, but a name my former roommates used when referring to Elena, guardian of the ground floor. She had an uncanny sense for when anyone was lingering at the hallway mailboxes, emerging from her cave ready to castigate.

Amber and I were her only company in the building one August night. When the power went out and we were caught without the fusebox key, we considered ignoring the problem and going to sleep. But downstairs we went, convinced a butter knife could work as a key substitute.

Not so much. My tear-smeared fingers were wedged in the crevice between the box door and the wall, while Amber maneuvered the knife in vain. Elena appeared, yelling operatically.

"You're making too much noise. What are you even doing with that wall?"

"My television's gone out! What have you two *done*?!"

Her television always puttered out whenever there was a power issue in our apartment. This was the basis of most of our hallway exchanges, even when everything was functioning just fine. She continued.

"You're making too much noise. What are you even doing with that wall?"

"Getting power back so you get your TV back. Please *abbia pazienza, la preghiamo.*"

By the time we'd ripped open the wall to find a purposeless compartment and no sign of the fusebox, it was clear she'd been yelling because the switches were overhead—and unlocked.

She agreed not to rat out our wall-ripping (we patched it up nicely) if we agreed to generally be less stupid.

In the absence of Mother, The Lady Downstairs knows best.

Sorry, I'm exhausted, going to bed. James is on the couch, but please lock him in the kitchen once you arrive.

Vol. 4

Significant others

For Daniel, details of {a person named} Florence's relationship with James were hazy prior to the whole group's arrival in {a city named} Florence.

Florence and Daniel had never met in person, but had arranged to split rent in a *quasi-quadrilocale* on sdrucciolo de' Pitti. Daniel was arriving from New Mexico for research. Florence had, for some time, been living in Florence, but was vacationing with James just before the new flat opened up.

Ciao, James and I've landed! See you soon, read her text to Daniel on move-in day.

This James character suddenly kept cropping up. Daniel didn't know Florence-the-person; deciding to live with her in Florence-the-city was already a gamble. She should still be in the Best-Flatmate-Foot-Forward period: why hadn't she mentioned a boyfriend? *A lease leech*, Daniel thought.

The irritation passed once some itinerary hiccups demanded Daniel's full attention. He would be arriving later than anticipated.

When he relayed the news to Florence, she seemed flexible. So did James, sort of: *We'll wait up! James is so excited he's jumping on the bed.*

Daniel tried to remember the terms for getting his deposit back.

A few hours later, his phone lit up again: *Sorry, I'm exhausted, going to bed. James is on the couch, but please lock him in the kitchen once you arrive.*

Squinting, Daniel read it a second time. Then a third. A swift follow-up message appeared before he could summon a polite way to ask what the hell this relationship was.

Don't worry, his litterbox is in there.

Vol. 5

Safe words

Rent had been due a few days, but Amber and I had time to find a fourth roommate to help us pay it. This was Florence. People needed rooms.

The August factor, however, hadn't figured in to our calculations. Things looked bleak on EasyStanza.it (a misnomer: *PiuttostoDifficileStanza* is more fitting, but packs less of a punch).

We were still mid-fantasy, fixated on the hope of a fourth BFF, someone cool and international who, ideally, enjoyed cleaning the bathroom. Our cocky certainty about the appeal of the *camera* never abated.

Enter our choices: 63-year old Boris*, with whom we did not entertain a visit, and student Melania*, whose profile suggested she *might not* be a serial killer. The gold standard in August.

Amber and I agreed, prior to Melania's visit, that we'd offer her the room on the spot, barring any *real* reservations either of us had. Since we couldn't slip off to whisper those mid-visit, we selected a "safe word" of sorts: "I think there's someone at the door." This would signal that one of us was unsure.

Melania, dressed uniformly in jet black, arrived forty minutes late, a camera slung around her neck. She neither acknowledged her tardiness nor spoke until Amber ventured, "Are you a photographer?" Her reply: "I fancy myself a bit of a hunter."

In unison, Amber and I turned to tend to an imaginary knock.

We exchanged token pleasantries, showed Melania the room, sent her home and shortly thereafter resumed breathing.

Minutes later an SMS arrived. "Thanks for the visit," Melania's words went. "The room's nice but I'm concerned about compatibility."

Perhaps Boris would like cleaning the bathroom, we told ourselves.

**names changed*

Vol. 6

UFOs

Neighborly interactions have increased exponentially for me since I made the jump (down) from a third-floor walk-up to a ground floor apartment. This is thanks to a phenomenon I rarely experienced in my years upstairs: UFOs (Unidentified Falling Objects).

The only UFO yet to be scientifically explained is a hot pink shoelace that landed on the rooftop covering over my garden. No one has come knocking, and it's not the sort of object for which one races to haul out the ladder. But that's relative. I'm slowly accepting that with ground floor power comes ground floor responsibility.

Recently, mid-morning dash, a note appeared under my door, detailing the drop of a sad white sneaker onto my garden's covering. There was a kind introduction, a request to come retrieve it and a phone number, which I promptly noted, planning to dial it later in the day—battery was low, I was late. I broom-fished the shoe off the roof and hid it in the condo hallway.

Two hours passed before I remembered. I zapped off an SMS about the shoe's whereabouts, we exchanged a few pleasantries and I considered the matter closed.

I returned home to another note: the same neighbor, perhaps surmising I couldn't read Italian, had gotten desperate in the two hours that elapsed between Note 1 and my reply. She'd photographed the shoe, printed it on a full 8x11 sheet, circled the sneaker with a magic marker and written beneath it "SORRY. MY SHOE IS IN YOUR GARDEN. PLEASE CALL ME."

Urgency is relative. I'm faster to fetch the ladder these days.

I zapped off an SMS about the shoe's whereabouts, we exchanged a few pleasantries and I considered the matter closed.

Do make sure your rent isn't too high, honey. No one wants to be house poor.

Vol. 7

Hidden awful things

Real estate is said to have three rules: location, location, location. Rents rise in fashionable areas—this is, of course, amplified in Florence. And, rather inconveniently for cash-strapped city dwellers, leading experts (okay, mothers) love to cite this saying, manipulating its original meaning: *Location is everything. Safety is paramount. Move across the ocean, sure, but by God, don't move into a Bad Neighborhood.*

Followed quickly by: *Do make sure your rent isn't too high, honey. No one wants to be house poor.*

Such difficult-to-reconcile sentiments have led some sons and daughters to give up and stick to a Bad Neighborhood budget.

Imagine my elation when I nabbed a flat in a decidedly Good Neighborhood, with a price tag typically reserved for Bads and basements. Still, a few days in at my new digs, the threat of the "HAT" loomed. (Coined by an ex-boss, the HAT is the fourth rule of real estate—the Hidden Awful Thing, bound to appear after enough months elapse).

Not enough natural light in the foyer, I reassured myself. *That's the "awful" thing*. Hardly hidden.

A visiting friend and I had barely popped the inaugural prosecco before he pointed out the structure's one eyesore, the fat orange pipe lining my ground floor garden's wall.

Not cute, I know, I'll cover it with a trellis or something like a real homeowner, I babbled. But he was distracted by the chorus of *whooshing* sounds from the apartments above, which I'd theretofore been unable to identify.

"Oh, great...you've got the *Poop Chute*!"

Neither plumbing peculiarities nor HATs is confined to Bad Neighborhoods.

Vol. 8

Takeover tenants

If you rent in Florence but don't expect to live your entire life in one palazzo, you will probably one day navigate the hurdles of early withdrawal from a housing contract.

One of these is pinning down a takeover tenant. The landlord, if amenable to your departure request, will delegate this task to you. It's fair enough, functioning as your "payment" for leaving sooner than you said you would.

Finding a takeover tenant will seem easy. Particularly if your apartment is well-priced, attractive and in a desirable location. But if it is all those things (in Florence, no less), you aren't moving.

Things will initially look promising. Friends will express enthusiasm for the room/flat/converted garage you're vacating. But once prompted to actually commit, their interest will prove as empty as the chorus of "*Ci vediamo presto*"'s sung among acquaintances at gatherings with free buffets.

This author got lucky. (So I thought.) My roommate fatigue flared up right as a friend decided she couldn't remain in her expensive (*one bed)Room with a view*. We'd pull off the perfect switch, *Strangers on a Train* style.

In retrospect it could only have been perfect if she'd been a stranger, period. Passing your place to a friend is the real estate equivalent of a lotus birth. Once-minor house issues are bound to snowball, and the guilt for getting out while you could will then creep in. Remotely invested in someone's happiness? He or she shouldn't be your takeover tenant.

It's not the Christian approach, perhaps, but there was that whole bit about showing hospitality to strangers. Just go ahead and hand the entire house over to them.

Vol. 9

Our sinks, our selves

In Flannery O'Connor's *A Good Man is Hard to Find*, a grandmother goes on a road trip. She wears her finest organdy garments so in case of an accident, "anyone seeing her dead on the highway would know at once that she was a lady."

We're supposed to be put off by her superficiality. Deep down, though, I know that similar safeguarding of my own self-image, in case of doomsday or unexpected guests, has always been the key force pushing me to wash my dishes.

Just-shy-of-squalor is my default mode, and it makes no sense: the stacks of dishes routinely left unattended by a roommate were what spurred me on to solo living.

But it's said we hate in others what we see in ourselves. I'd mastered my own dish-degenerate impulses and couldn't bear such bad influence. It reminded me I was perpetually one skipped salad bowl away from ruin.

My prompt tending to the dishes, then, was a triumph—until recently, when my landlady stopped by on short notice. A Galluzzo native of a certain age, she oozes an impossible mix of housewifely know-how and career-gal chutzpah. I'm eager to impress her.

Surveying the flat, she exclaimed, "No one has ever kept it this clean!"

I beamed. But then she entered the kitchen. "It's almost like you *don't even use it*!"

Since then, my "sink=self" priorities have shifted. I leave something to soak each night for posterity, aware of my high risk of relapse. But in this country, a sink with one soapy saucepan and a few stray forks is a benign sign of life well-lived.

If I'm knocked over by an ATAF bus on the *viale*, at least Florentines will know at once that I cooked.

Vol. 10

Neighborhood loyalties

From the period of November 2016 to April 2017 I was positively desperate and, as a result, insufferable. You will read that and perhaps link it to a certain orange-tinged election, but the primary culprit was the housing market in Florence.

My search was all I could talk about (hence the creation of this column). In the initial month, I made quite a production of broadcasting my hope to end up on my very same street (in hindsight—ha!) Switching neighborhoods after three years of befriending shopkeepers, baristas and finally choosing between the road's two butchers? *No thanks*, I fussed, to anyone who'd listen.

But the shopkeeper bit was kind of a sham. Sure, I favored certain corners and familiar faces, but my only real loyalty was to my *vino sfuso* supplier.

In presentations to potential housemates, it was a prime selling point—or I framed it that way, anyway. Wine on tap just two doors down? Who wouldn't sign up? Over time, all our visitors—Dutch and German parents of roommates, colleagues, dates—were routinely impressed (worried?) by the cork collection we'd amassed from near-daily walks to the watering hole.

The shop owner himself knew of my search and even some of my parameters. One of them, though he had no idea, was actually "within walking distance of this shop", which later evolved to "within walking distance of a similar business" and finally "within walking distance of Florence at all."

I did end up with one of said "similar businesses" on my new block, and the first shop permanently shut down in the very period I moved away. Coincidence or not, I can't quite shake the guilt, but I only really talk about it when drinking. *In vino, veritas.*

Vol. 11

Tutto incluso

Tutto incluso. "All-inclusive."

What a difference these two words make in a housing listing. Having the costs of water, gas, electricity—and in certain otherworldly apartments, WiFi—factored in to a flat's monthly rate is usually a rich-landlord ruse. Still, it's one many of us would happily tolerate. Costs as a tenant in a *tutto incluso* system can be higher, but it's a small tradeoff for the ease of no post office legwork, no meter-reading, no calls from utility companies. Knowing precisely what's in your pocket each month? Priceless.

But in Florence, we run into a real estate variation on one infamous Orwell theme: "All *tutto incluso* rents include 'everything', but some include more 'everything' than others." I'm reminded of a friend who was wooed by a listing for a furnished apartment with *tutto incluso* tacked on at the end. Upon visiting, she discovered *tutto incluso* just meant the pictured furniture was part of the deal.

Never trust an ad with no bullet-points of bills under the *tutto* umbrella.

The very existence of *tutto incluso* setups can also cause confusion for negligent landlords. My "takeover tenant" (see RD vol. 8) is in a space where nothing is *incluso*, yet all utilities remain in the owner's name; she assumed it was a convenience-based decision on his part. Cluelessness is the more probable explanation. By all appearances, he seems to think they set a *tutto incluso* rate, though the flat's base rent remains fixed as it ever was. Someone—we're not sure who—has been paying the takeover tenant's bills over the past year and a half, since no power outages nor heating halts have transpired. All signs point to bad math or a property manager gone rogue, but I guess we'll never really know *tutto*.

Vol. 12

Business ideas

In an exercise of sound judgment, the powers-that-be here at *The Florentine* recently barred me from posting photographs I've taken on *TF*'s channels without first consulting him. I mean them. Okay, there's just one power that be, at least when it comes to visuals. (His name is Marco.) Photography is, to put it mildly, not my forte.

Still, despite my utter lack of lens know-how, I'm convinced there's room for me to make real money as a photographer, crushing the competition to boot. It's all about breaking into the right arena: apartment ads.

I should mention that I already have a pro bono side gig as a sympathetic real estate agent for soon-to-be-homeless friends. Scouring housing listings, upturning bar bulletin board leaflets to uncover steals scribbled on sticky notes—these happen to be favorite pastimes. Thus I'm well-acquainted with the average photos placed alongside flat descriptions. The bar is lower than the lowest *seminterrato* this side of the sea.

The bar is lower than the lowest seminterrato *this side of the sea.*

Presumably, these ad posters—usually agencies—want to get these apartments rented. But the accompanying photographs feel...oddly salacious, like a real estate version of "Stars without makeup!" They often seem accidental, as if someone inadvertently tapped an iPhone's home button mid-save, just before the screen hit the floor. Zoom-ins on thoroughly unremarkable room corners; intimate close-ups of IKEA lightbulbs; flash-happy bathroom mirror shots, often with the bonus of a lurking reflection; and a personal favorite, views out the window, usually of internal condo walls or a blurry sky. Helpful.

How these ads attract tenants is astonishing, but city-wide desperation—compliments of a certain vacation rental giant—must generate traction. Strangely, the photos are a comforting reminder that Florence is not one giant B&B. I think I'll shelve my business idea for now.

I ignored the bell, since only serial killers ring bells after 10pm.

Vol. 13

Things that bug me

You might remember a scene in *Annie Hall* that takes place after the titular character and Alvy Singer have parted ways. Alvy receives a frantic 3am phone call, rushing across the city for Annie's purported emergency. He is incredulous to learn it's just a spider in the bathroom.

Annie and the women of 1977 were Liberated™, but I hold this truth to be self-evident: not even Judith Butler relishes the chance to squash a spider. The letting-men-kill-the-bugs thing is a gender role relic that frankly doesn't ruffle my feminist feathers. I'm happy to hurl them my independently purchased Raid can while I tend to our bigger battles.

I experienced a peculiarly Florentine version of this phenomenon, though, after our condo administrator alerted tenants of a cockroach invasion. Many of us hadn't noticed, since the vile little rascals blended in with the pebbled floor.

It was Wednesday, midnight. Wearing my (literal) grandmother's nightgown, I was petting my excitable pup when the doorbell rang, and he let out your requisite yap or six. (His daily don't-bark-at-the-doorbell training consists in me gently reminding him of city noise ordinances, a method I'm soon to patent.)

I ignored the bell, since only serial killers ring bells after 10pm. But through the peephole I spotted my upstairs neighbor, a nice young father with whom I've probably exchanged four words. *HE's the killer?* Calming down once I saw he was clutching a broom, I opened the door.

"Sorry for the *disturbo*," he said, his eyes jumping between the grandma gown and babbling furball. "But I was out here killing cockroaches, and I saw one crawl under your door." Then he walked away.

Perhaps I'm old fashioned. But I was baffled as to why a relative stranger would ring at midnight to share such information, gawk at his neighbor's nightwear, rile up her dog and then fail to deliver. The knight in shining armor showed up, but dropped the ball. Or in this case, the broom. Mercifully, I buy my own Raid.

Vol. 14

La privacy

Now that we—in the EU, at least—are all sick of the GDPR and would gift Lucifer our cookie consent on a Christmas tray if it meant the *link would just go straight to the stupid article*, our short-term memory as a society is rusty.

Remember the inspiring uprising in the immediate Cambridge Analytica aftermath, when grand plans were being made to topple the Zuckerbourgeoisie? The rage turned tepid once we collectively decided we'd rather follow Jenna from high school's weight loss journey than seize the means of production. (But speaking of production, have you seen Jenna's grain bowls?)

Cambridge Analytica is now defunct, but I like to imagine how things might have turned out if the firm had downsized and rehabbed its image by relocating. Had I been in charge of putting out the PR fires, I'd have advised them to move HQ to my Florence condo, where their data-culling methods would have seemed amateur—even pure—by my building's standards. *La privacy* was a lost cause in Tuscan rental flats long before targeted Facebook ads were ever born.

I touched on *la privacy* (or lack thereof) in RD vol. 6, explaining how renting a ground floor flat with a modest garden has meant a surge in notes, sheepish knocks and window shouts from neighbors, all thanks to UFOs (Unidentified Falling Objects) that land on my turf. But in terms of concrete evidence of the privacy lacking in Florentine living, the U-F-O, I've learned, is no match for the D-O-G.

Adopting one is the fastest way to get (too) familiar with your fellow tenants, your landlord and that gray-haired gentleman in the next building over who's perpetually lurking in the window. It's also an eye-opening lesson in how much this crew has actually seen, overheard or inferred all along.

I once naïvely cashed in my third-floor neighbor's offer to walk my dog when I couldn't make it home on my lunch break; by 3.30pm, my phone was buzzing again. "I see you're not home yet," she wrote. "Want me to take him out a second time?" I said no. One guard dog was enough.

Then there was the sole party of last summer—a pre-pup affair and the One I Thought I Got Away With. A Saturday farewell shindig for my dearest friend, it continued well past quiet hours, but wrapped up without incident and was never repeated. Yet now, a year later, with a dog in the picture, it's my omniscient landlady's kingpin, the trump card dealt to shut down all debate with me. *"But you had a party!"* is my own personal *"But her emails!"*

Sadly, my party had no servers, private or otherwise.

Vol. 15

What-ifs

Sex and the City's writing-by-the-window sage "couldn't help but wonder" about a lot of things, rarely speaking in the cadence of certainty. One of the exceptions was her oft-quoted proclamation that New Yorkers are "always looking for a job, a boyfriend, or an apartment." If the shiny story arcs are to be believed, early-2000s Manhattanites hunted for each with targeted efficiency, enabled by Blackberries, gallery openings, and only writing one column per week.

Many transplants to Florence are similarly on the lookout for those three anchoring forces that can clinch the deal. But—and don't fall off your chair, now—as a group, we are a little less practical and expedient.

Hack it here long-term and you'll notice that jobs and partners often appear through the combined currents of accident and evolution. Apartments, meanwhile, must be aggressively researched, seized, camped outside—approached with the belligerence of Jordan Belfort (or Samantha Jones, to stay on-theme). Even in 2018, only rookies, masochists, and new money expats can reasonably confine their searches to the Internet. *Vis-à-vis* exchanges and vaguely predatory behavior are key for the rest of us.

One caveat to this tenacious, Manhattan-style treatment of the search: in Florence, it only works with places already on the market. In every chat I have with house hunting friends and acquaintances—is it normal to average two per week?—I feel burdened by the weight of the inexplicably empty first-floor flat above me. *To mention or not to mention*? It's been unoccupied since long before I landed here, but the unhurried owners do seem haphazardly interested in renovating and renting it when I remind them it exists.

Deceitful. That's how I feel sitting on (well, under) such a secret when Florence's market is so dire. Yet bringing it up and passing off the owner contact is a false lead, sure to evaporate sooner than what was said during a late July meeting or what was written on a naked form (the kind with no *marca da bollo* affixed).

And in the interest of full transparency, the raging narcissist in me—I did clock a lot of time with Carrie Bradshaw in my formative years, after all— does kind of enjoy dispensing this non-tip. There's the dopamine rush when someone gasps in gratitude, the fleeting existential satisfaction of appearing relevant, well-connected. Knowing all the while, of course, that I can default to "just the messenger" when it inevitably leads nowhere.

Still. Yet. Biting my tongue seems the smart thing to do. The empty apartment is spacious, light-filled and probably the same price as mine. New Yorker I am not, but programmed to gun for upgrades, yes. Is there a chance that, Florentine-style, some collision of happy accidents will cause a renovation to happen in my lifetime? *I can't help but wonder*.

Vis-à-vis *exchanges and vaguely predatory behavior are key for the rest of us.*

Sometimes in this town, you just need to look at a leaf.

Vol. 16

Concessions

On Facebook recently, an acquaintance put out one of those pseudo-“ask the audience” posts. You know the kind: ostensibly the person wants input, but really their mind is quite made up, so while waiting for the 14 bus, or for their pasta water to boil, they pose a question and hope a few of their 1,100 “friends” will throw them a validating bone. (So, most Facebook posts, really.)

His was a dilemma he faced as a prospective homebuyer. An affordable apartment in central Florence, or just on its fringes, had no balcony but was otherwise perfect. His question: was this *truly* a dealbreaker?

Given my interest in all things real estate, I scrolled through the comments voyeuristically, though the subject was about as juicy as drywall. Two schools of thought emerged among the commenters, but with a shared consensus: a concession or two is always necessary. It’s up to the buyer to decide which ones are workable.

Home buying happens on an island I won’t visit for some time, but I nonetheless have strong opinions on the balcony-slash-outdoor-space matter.

Even as a renter, my one non-negotiable in my last search was an outdoor space of some kind (be it a garden or a *balconcino* that could barely hold an herb pot.) Creative solutions can fix things like a view of the fridge from the bed, but in congested Florence, a "personal piazza", however small, is priceless, and can't just be added at will. Plus, sometimes in this town, you just need to look at a leaf.

The Facebook post's pro-balcony camp strangely mentioned nothing of how such a space, regardless of its dimensions, can make a flat feel double its size. How it offers simultaneous respite from and engagement with the city. They were relentless realists, these commenters, asking the poster where he'd hang his laundry, or where he'd chuck trash bags with storms looming and willpower lacking.

It got me thinking about a revealing aspect of my own raised-ground floor balcony, the threshold to my ~~dog WC~~ garden and perhaps to my psyche. While the garden is a picturesque "personal piazza" in its finest hours, the balcony is best identified as laundry and trash purgatory. My skivvies, barely-coping herbs and bags of kitchen scraps sit brazenly out where my ideal self would hang fairy lights and flowers; my real self›s charming substitutes are partially obscured by a covering, but ultimately in plain view for anyone in the palazzo who bothers looking hard enough. (Meanwhile, I pretend not to be home if a neighbor rings my bell unexpectedly and my apartment isn't 100 percent pristine.)

No cell reception inside means if I work from home, the balcony is my call center; I regularly waltz onto it with wet hair, wearing a bathrobe. But I never take the full two steps down into the garden in such circumstances. I can concede to basic decorum.

Vol. 17

The blondes upstairs

My first year and a half or so in Italy was spent grasping at any sort of anchoring point. For a brief period in this trial-by-fire, I bunked—"lived" would be pushing it—in a sterile shared apartment where an IKEA fruit bowl was the closest thing we had to décor. This bowl was perpetually empty, or worse, would have a single browning apple sitting in it.

Graduating to a four-bedroom walk-up with three friends, two succulents and some matching plates, then, was a thrill. On my first day in this exciting new building, I bumped into Elena, the ground floor's lone resident (see RD vol. 3). She was a condo version of the village elder, as indispensable to the palazzo's architecture as the stairs or ceilings.

Wanting to seem neighborly and naively not able to read her raised eyebrows, I extended a hand and introduced myself, to which she responded, "Oh, *cara*, that's sweet, but I'm never going to remember your name."

Fair enough. Further comments from her helped me gather that our top floor flat had indeed always been a revolving door of "*ragazze biondine*," as she put it.

At that stage of my life, I hadn't yet felt that fatigue that sets in after one hears enough Joe Fiorentinos throw all foreigners into the same sack, without regard for depth of roots, command of Italian, dexterity in the kitchen. If you've read this far, you likely know that fatigue, and have learned to brush it off and pick your battles when you meet a Joe.

Elena, though, was not "Joe Fiorentino". Not even Gioia, really: just aging and wonderfully frank.

My then-landlord, who recently resurfaced after a nearly two-year silence, is a different story. Before I moved out—bidding goodbye to Elena and life with roommates—I'd contacted him a reasonable amount of times in an attempt to procure my Final Balance Due on around two months' worth of utilities. Crickets! I'd have been a loon to keep pushing for this after four or five attempts.

Well, my takeover tenant (see RD vol. 8)—a friend who moved into my old room and has also since abandoned ship—recently got the brunt of this when the silent landlord suddenly reared his head, casually requesting close to three years' worth of bill payments in a lump sum, with no breakdown, consideration of individual tenants' timelines, or indication of how it was to work. In this situation, she went to the contract.

Within the first paragraph it was clear that each time our Joe re-registered it with the new tenants' names, he hadn't bothered to change the data. Her name was indeed in the contract, but was accompanied by my birthplace. A former roommate's *codice fiscale*. Myriad other never-trimmed traces of the many *ragazze biondine* (and even some brunettes) who'd occupied the apartment. Contractual pandemonium.

For him, we really were all the same. But it's to be expected: as we learned, he likes to operate in lump sums.

Vol. 18

Handymen

I grew up attending an Episcopal church in Mississippi, which felt a bit like swimming on the moon. Our priest once remarked in a sermon that if a Mississippian hears someone say she's from New York City, he'll respond along these lines: "Oh, I have a friend there. Do you know *x*?"

The maddening and inescapable Magnolia state is more like a club than a region. At least that's the description I once heard in Florence from the former rector of Saint James, a fellow Southerner, now newly repatriated. It's largely true, if one grows up or plants roots among moon-swimmers. But most of us *do* learn that projecting the Mississippi club concept onto large swaths of people is at best naïve ("I know this person in New York, do you?") and at worst offensive ("You're *x*, do you know my friend who's also *x*?")

Post-adolescence, in marginally more cosmopolitan environments, I had to do a lot of un-learning of such six degrees of Kevin Bacon-and-grits tendencies. So imagine my surprise when, a few years into renting in Florence, I started noticing a pattern that didn't appear very PC to point out: all my Florentine handymen seemed to know each other.

"Handymen" here is no euphemism for anything exciting. I mean the workers who have variously helped resolve my running toilet trial, leaking hot water heater, and oppressively tangled jasmine vines.

Before you call me daft, I do realize that most property owners provide tenants with a list of their preferred plumber, electrician, gardener, you name it—and that as such, a sort of favored-Mr.-Fix-It fraternity might emerge over time. This was abundantly clear years ago, when my first long-term landlord refused to foot bills for any messes cleaned up by not-his-guys.

Still, I've witnessed considerable "club" patterns even outside the inner circles shaped by landlord-prescribed speed dial lists. In my current place, just before Christmas, a hot water heater leak showed up in one of those slow-to-manifest domestic crises with a series of domino effects. Said effects—including a lack of power—made it challenging, first to identify the root issue, and later, to get a man. On the phone. Hence I deviated from my rental's Rolodex.

The *caldaia* warrior who came through was a lone wolf, with no apparent links to my flat's associated fraternity. When he determined we'd need reinforcement from a plumber, he phoned the very same saint who'd assisted me months earlier when a water bill wiped out most of my savings. Perhaps he's just the best in the business, but their call and subsequent repair session were peppered with the easy banter of semi-brotherhood, long-term friendship simmered over decades.

If you live in Florence and are not particularly handy, you've probably seen similar dynamics amid household disasters. Or maybe you have just one go-to person—you know a guy. Well, so does he. Join the club.

Vol. 19

Serious

Not to toot my own horn or anything, but in the sixth grade I almost nabbed first place at my school's spelling bee. (Please hold your applause until the end, thanks.) Panicked by what such a prize might mean for my social standing, I purposely fumbled at the last second, omitting the "e" in "hearth". Cringe-worthy, yes, but likeability was everything then, and academic ambition carried no weight with the cool kids.

It took years for me to stop tempering my tenacity. Today I have no qualms about "admitting" that my competitive drive is alive and kicking, but the ghost of that insecure sixth grader still likes to turn up now and then.

Two years ago in Florence, she cost me—wouldn't you know it—a hearth. More precisely, an affordable one-bedroom with a tease of a fireplace and floozy of a terrace. See, I went on a group visit to a renovated rental, newly on the market in a sought-after neighborhood. I'd been herded upstairs with a dozen other hopefuls after arriving to the address and wondering what they were doing at my visit.

Like everyone else, I piped up and left my details, but kind of knew it was a lost cause.

Bearing documents and *buste paga*, I'd come ready to sign on-site. I'd also dimly assumed the agent would walk me through alone. Instead, competition was cutthroat: nearly everyone else was part of a couple with two paychecks. One woman was pregnant. The lone single guy in the group was, heartbreakingly, a young widower, desperate to leave the place he'd shared with his wife. So he said, anyway.

The place itself was absurdly, irritatingly perfect, and the agent knew this; she seemed to enjoy it. We circled back to the front door, group-gazing at the space like Davids on Bathshebas, dogs on bones, Florence residents on 600-euro *bilocali*. "*Allora*," the agent began, playing dumb, "if anyone's interested..."

Like everyone else, I piped up and left my details, but kind of knew it was a lost cause. I could have cornered the agent again after the group dispersed, but the sixth grade part of my soul was a little too timid, a smidge convinced that somehow, she was undeserving. (Plus, the pregnant girl refused to budge. She might very well have stayed until her water broke.)

I got home and sent an email, left a voicemail, lit a votive candle. Called again the next morning and it was clear I wouldn't advance to the next round of the rental bee. "Four people from last night are here in my office right now," barked the agent. "I only want serious offers. Are you coming or what?"

Now and again I do wonder what might have been had I acted more ruthless. I've got spunk, to be sure. But living here—indeed, just living—requires such stamina. Sometimes it's simply not in me to be serious and obstinate about *every single thing*.

Spelling, though, is another matter entirely.

The building's ground-floor grandma who lived rent-free and took no prisoners wouldn't have abided this.

Vol. 20

Comebacks

Have you ever had "comeback sauce"? Originating in the American South, like your author, it's a spicy catch-all (ketch-all?) condiment, a dubious blend of mayo, paprika, garlic and chili sauce, spooned onto bland salads or used to amp up fried pickles. It's also the image—and taste—that springs to mind and tongue when, about once a decade, I summon the gall to sass anyone in power. *Boom.* Comeback sauce.

Pigheaded with family and close friends, I nonetheless shrink to Little Bo No-Peep in disagreements with authority figures. Landlords in Florence, particularly. It's a product of actively resisting the "fussy foreigner" peg; as technical guests, however long-term, we want to be courteous, to accept things at face value. A mostly healthy attitude to keep, sure, but when patiently tolerating a glaringly negligent landlord, it's easy to self-lobotomize and say you're "just adapting." But we can't kid ourselves. When it counts, you've got to be able to cut the grateful-Italy-ingénue stuff and scrap like a *nonna* in line at the supermarket.

In my first longer-term Florentine apartment, I saw my landlord once—*maybe* twice—in three and a half years, justifying his behavior because, hey, we had a view of Boboli.

Severe piping issues arose one summer in our kitchen and bathroom; the sinks fell out of commission, rendering the whole downstairs unusable. Sauce-stained plates and fond-riddled pots counter-camped for a week till it dawned on my roommates and me that we could hose them down on the terrace. Unable to cook, to flush, we watched our food expenses triple, our working toilets get halved. Why didn't we make more of a stink (so to speak?) Call plumbers ourselves, complain to the owner? We did both, constantly. But, to explain in highly scientific terms: Ferragosto week + gasp-inducing estimates ÷ lack of cash to cover emergency without reimbursement = landlord's refusal to agree to anything before his September 10 return.

The building's ground-floor grandma who lived rent-free and took no prisoners wouldn't have abided this. She stopped me by the mailboxes one morning, as was her way, to rail about her television, the mold creeping into her bathroom and the refusal of the palazzo's lead goon—a polite rephrasing of what she termed him—to check in on anyone, anytime, least of all August. As I filled her in on his latest shortcoming, she noted that yet another (Italian) family had moved out from the floor that separated us.

Her allyship and anger sparked an epiphany: expecting the most basic level of occasional house maintenance, and happening to be foreign, does not equate to *you* being "high maintenance". Sucking in my breath, I drafted an email slathered in comeback sauce and *congiuntivo*. In ten minutes my rent refund demand had been shut down, but I'd taken my tenant agency back. He'd conceded to cover the repairs, plus a food allowance.

Adapting sometimes looks like keeping your head down, staying kind, humble. But now and then—probably more than once a decade, really—it should also mean emulating the ninja *nonne* you know.

Vol. 21

The palazzo philharmonic

Hello, my name is Mary, and I'm not an alcoholic (I don't think). But if I am one thing, I am categorically unable to keep wine glasses from shattering into tiny pieces on my rental apartment's marble floors. It happens loudly, and often, and with impressively vigorous resolve on the part of the stemware.

Strange, not easily identifiable noises from strange, easily identifiable neighbors are part of the deal when you sign up for condominium living. They're just as common as the crying babies, barking dogs and bumbling party guests we all expect will be part of the lineup at some point or another. A noise, for me, is "strange"—distinct from the more standard Florentine symphony—only when inscrutable. Was that the snort of a sleep apnea-afflicted *nonno*? The coo of a pigeon or the muffled voice of Maria De Filippi trickling down from a fourth floor TV?

These mysteries are far more perplexing than those connected to concretely nameable sounds (case in point: a deadened doorbell rings faintly each time I close my palazzo's *portone*. Nobody is ever buzzing, but the door-belody plays out each time, unfailingly, over the percussion-like *click* of the latch. The sound is unmistakably a doorbell, even if deadened, and therefore cannot qualify as strange).

What I cannot know for sure, especially given the weird insulation of our building, is how the operatic glass smashing sounds from outside *my* four walls—whether it is now considered my irritating but predictable contribution to the palazzo philharmonic. Alternatively, perhaps these ear-grating noises are untraceable, and therefore *strange;* a welcome fuel, in other words, for the condominium's collective imagination.

I suppose I could ask my neighbors about it (just the ones whose noises I can squarely identify, to give me ammunition against potential complaints. "People who live in glass houses shouldn't throw stones" and all that). But maybe they'll clap back and say that people who live on marble floors shouldn't throw glasses.

Vol. 22

Rear Window experiences

My mother calls something a "*Rear Window* experience" when it fails to live up to great expectations ("I'm excited to take you to this restaurant. Sure hope it's not a *Rear Window* experience"). She's never gotten over the time she force-fed my younger sister and me the Hitchcock classic—after much, much buildup—and our teenaged selves failed to be dazzled by James Stewart's and Grace Kelly's tense, two-hour verbal tennis match. We were whiny and eye-roll-y and eager for *something to happen already*.

Several years later at university, I took a Hitchcock course from a teacher who was not my mother, and *Rear Window*—go figure—suddenly morphed into the most brilliant movie I'd ever seen. (Sorry Mama, you're always right, et cetera). The movie was the crux of the syllabus and I grew obsessed with its witty screenplay, glamorous costuming and subtle critiques of condo-facilitated voyeurism.

I think of the film often in my ground floor Florence apartment, which was rented to me "partially furnished"—the sweet spot for foreign-born people with 4+4 contracts. (It means you can forego things like Byzantine Jesus prints in the boudoir, but don't have to buy your own refrigerator.) A hobbit-sized coffee table was included with my partially furnished flat; fun little extras like a bed and curtains to cover the street-facing window were not.

Due to a lethal combination of aesthetic indecision and what *Buzzfeed*'s Anne Helen Petersen termed "errand paralysis", I've still not bothered to buy and hang window treatments. Any view inside my place is obstructed by sunlight (or shutters, come nightfall). In moments of passing paranoia, though, I imagine a boredom-ridden, binocular-toting, wheelchair-bound Giacomo Stewart watching across the way, waiting to implicate me in a murder. Sadly, if I do have a Tuscan peeping Tommaso, I've been a pretty boring study of late: sorting laundry, petting my dog or, in the wildest of worst-case scenarios, falling asleep before closing shutters and clicking off lights. Watching me would be a "*Rear Window* experience", basically. From the front.

Vol. 23

Tidying up

I had dinner last night with an old friend and onetime Florence housemate, someone who inspires envy quite easily: ritzy job in Rome, gorgeous wardrobe, adoring *fidanzato*. Even though we lived together briefly, she's still the kind of person I imagine sleeps on a cloud, remembers to toss lavender sachets in the laundry, and keeps her place ready for a photography troupe from *Architectural Digest* at all times. But when the subject of cleaning our respective rentals came up (I was in the middle of a marathon weekend session), she confessed she lives in constant fear of knocks from the neighbors or landlord. "I hear footsteps pitter-pattering in the hallway," she said, "and my first thought is, 'Where can I throw everything?!'"

As someone who's ignored a few doorbell rings in her day—hiding from readers of the water meter, usually, or rerouting packages to inconvenient locations out of shame—I took comfort in this. I like to pretend I enjoy cleaning, but the truth is I enjoy having a clean house.

I like to pretend I enjoy cleaning, but the truth is I enjoy having a clean house.

The latter unfortunately can't materialize without the former. Sometimes cleaning sounds fun, cathartic even. But once I start, I remember that what's fun and cathartic is pouring a glass of wine, putting on *Rumours* and sort of pushing a broom around. Not gloves-on, grout-targeting labor.

Luckily, my across-the-hall neighbors, a family of three, would probably not pass judgment if they had to stop by my place spontaneously. At the very least, they'd empathize with the struggle of keeping it primed for surprise visitors. I know this because I got locked out of the apartment one day last August with a visiting friend and my dog; we were auto-banished to the condo hallway during a summer storm.

The careless choice I'd made to leave my garden-facing back door unlocked ended up saving us: we determined we wouldn't have to call the fire department or the landlady (same thing, really) if we could *just* climb out of the third-floor communal window and scale the wall down into my garden. This plan got quite far along before it occurred to us that we could simply walk through the neighbors' apartment, exit into their garden, and cross over into mine. They needed to be home, though—this was crucial.

In perfect theatrical timing, the husband walked in the front door, shaking out his rain jacket and jumping at the sight of the three stooges perched on the condo stairs. We explained politely, matter-of-factly, that we could perhaps avoid causing an international incident if he could please let us walk through his apartment and into the garden to get back inside via the back door, and *he wouldn't mind, would he, we've been concocting wild plans but ha ha ha, the solution is laughably simple, isn't it*?

But then I saw it on his face: the sheer panic that only an impromptu visit from a water meter reader or locked-out neighbor can inspire. The sudden appearance above his head of a real-life thought bubble, comic strip-style, with "WHERE CAN I THROW EVERYTHING?!" penciled inside of it would hardly have surprised me.

Catching on, I suggested an (ingenious) alternative. *He* would walk through his own apartment, his own garden, my garden, and then my door. My apartment was spotless; I had a planned visitor staying with me, so you could say I had a leg up.

Vol. 24

Training

At the start of our senior year of high school, my friend Anna and I discovered we'd neglected to earn the gym credits required to graduate. In a kind of accelerated recovery process, we were forced to enroll in Weightlifting with half of the Golden Wave, Tupelo High's middling football team. Our class met daily at 7am and was run by a man called Coach Funk, who wore zip-off track pants and told us on the first day that he'd "loved high school so much he'd never wanted to leave."

Anna and I managed okay, largely because Coach Funk stationed us at the bench press closest to the exit. Being outside his field of vision, we could mime our way through the warmups and spend the rest of the morning doing the previous night's homework for classes that, you know, had homework. Could we lift more than a textbook? No, but we got *really* good at letting commotion melt into white noise.

We memorized flash card-Spanish as metal barbells clattered onto concrete floors and Coach Funk jeered at the benchwarmers. We churned out five-paragraph essays on *Lord of the Flies* as real-life adolescent boys derided each other's virility all around us.

I can't say that in my years in Florence I've ever been reminded of Coach Funk, weightlifting class, or my onetime ability to tune out grating noises and get work done. Until a recent Friday at 7am. The apartment directly above mine has long been empty and uninhabitable, but that morning, I heard an end-of-the-world *thud* and an eruption of male voices that gave me Tupelo High gym flashbacks broken up by Florentine expletives. Peering into the hallway, I spotted a grim-looking notice taped by the mailboxes; any document that begins with "*Spettabile Condominio*", as you'll know, always spells trouble. This one announced that a crew was beginning work on installing new plumbing and electricity systems in the apartment upstairs. *Expected duration of renovations: 60 days.* So, 200, give or take.

The timing is comically bad, as I've just begun working from home. Turns out when you make that transition, regular old writer's block transforms into freelancer's shock—at how disturbing the quiet can be, how alone with your thoughts you can sometimes feel. Hearing the daily drop-and-drill rituals of this crew of Coach Funk-like Florentines feels like a sure enough pendulum swing. It's unfortunate I can't summon the sound-canceling concentration of my 17-year-old self, now that I'm older and my work is harder. But maybe this will be good training, the way weightlifting is supposed to be. I still sit close to the exit for when it gets to be too much.

Vol. 25

Collecting

By the time this column is printed, this is likely to be old news, but file the intel away for future reference. It seems that the Bellini Gallery—that antiques-filled, Arno-facing jewel of a building—is currently on a Marie Kondo kick. I say this based on the boxes of dusty coffee table books now sitting curbside for collection.

Last night, while inattentively walking my dog past the gallery, I glanced down to catch him marking on a weathered, water-stained Sotheby's catalog from the '70s, caught between a car tire and a hard place. My instinct was to scold him, but when I spotted the overstuffed cardboard box that must have once held the catalog—amongst other treasures—I realized that if anyone needed to be scolded, it was whoever dared throw all those out. A textbook-like treatise on Santa Maria del Carmine and a weighty hunker on Simone Martini and the Sienese school were among the scores I ended up taking home.

I've always been a collector: Beanie Babies, books, nail polishes, other people's unwanted stuff. A year or so ago, feeling jazzed about a golden frame I sourced near a bus stop, I texted my best friend across the ocean. (He's a former Florence resident who never sits on his bed in his "outside clothes", as he calls all clothes that aren't freshly laundered prince pajamas.)

You're going to kill me—but guess what!

Within ten seconds, he replied knowingly: *Did you find garbage on the street and bring it into your nice clean house? Mary, it's garbage for a reason.*

Despite what they say about "sparking joy," people like Marie Kondo and my friend love to rain on my kind's parade by criticizing our, er, collecting habits. I get it. The aspirational version of my décor style is "*Bobo in Paradise* who wishes she were Parisian". The actual version is more like "manic magpie with a touch of Miss Havisham". Few things are worse, though, than a sterile or IKEA-only rental, and few cities are better for ~~dumpster diving~~ curbside antiquing than Florence.

I have found kindred spirits, many of them local, mostly in the dark recesses of Instagram. Fashion influencers tag the labels they're wearing in their photos so you can "shop the look". If I tried doing that on shots of my living room, I'd be tagging a whole lot of nameless stoops, charity bazaars and junk hawkers whose hands have never once produced a *scontrino*. And, yes, probably more than a few ALIA bins.

Fellow Florentine upcyclers and I all avoid renting overly furnished apartments, lest we end up trapped with a Tuscan *nonna* aesthetic. The irony is we end up assembling a home full of their hand-me-downs and throw-me-outs anyway. But collecting is a time-honored pastime in this town. We all have our ways of taking part.

Vol. 26

Sitcoms

In the past week, I've had a particularly dense concentration of deadlines and a growing list of ungratifying errands to be run. In the past week, I also reactivated my Netflix subscription, because the need to binge-watch *Friends* chronologically suddenly became urgent. I can't imagine why.

Don't worry. Despite the rent-centric title of this column, I'm not going to harp on about the economic implausibility of Monica's apartment as if that's a creative thesis. I'm more interested in the ease with which the *Friends* glide in and out of Monica's apartment, juxtaposed with the (relative) lack of random folks who ring her doorbell. Monica Geller and I may share initials and insecurities, but if a sitcom existed with my Florence apartment as the anchor set, it wouldn't be called *Friends* (though I do have some, thanks for asking). A more realistic title would be *Random Folks Dropping in Unannounced.*

No one is obliged to answer the doorbell every time it rings, and I don't.

Since switching to self-employment from an office job, I've learned that sunlight hours in a ground floor Florence apartment bring an all-day parade of doorbell ringers. Door-to-door marketers; postal workers and water meter readers (they get a pass); prospective building buyers looking for Airbnb flips; Jehovah's Witnesses; people who want me to switch from Enel to Eni; people who *have* switched from Enel to Eni and are now going around proselytizing about it, presumably to keep the Jehovah's witnesses on their toes.

No one is obliged to answer the doorbell every time it rings, and I don't. But I am astounded at the frequency, and at how brazen most people are, particularly those with sales agendas. They're not flopping on the couch *a la* Joey Tribbiani, at least not without a pleading "*permesso?*" first. But by and large, they are unconcerned about taking up the time of anyone who dares open the door. And we ground floor-bound suckers get bit first.

The *Friends*-y level of casual expectation baked into these interactions always perplexes me. The daytime buzzers launch directly into their spiels, not processing how bizarre it is that we're ten feet from where I sleep, not pausing to consider that I might be on my way to meet the crew at Central Perk. (Er, Giubbe Rosse). Like the non-Monicas on *Friends,* none of the characters on *Random Folks Dropping in Unannounced* are ever surprised or delighted that I opened the door. My interactions with them have become what congregating at Monica's was for the gang: not *occasions,* but nonchalant, intimate exchanges, free of social niceties and contingent upon my being home.

The crucial difference is that good friends (and *Friends*) are allowed to strip things of pretense. Truth is, I always wanted a home where loved ones floated in and out as they pleased, and I cherish the kind of closeness where friends can gather without the gloss of *occasion*. But no Eni salespeople are on my Christmas list yet, so shouldn't they still be laying the social niceties on thick? Or at least feign delight when the door gets answered at 3pm on a Tuesday.

Vol. 27

Running gags

I don't tend to think of Phil Dunphy and Clark Griswold, the dopey dads of *Modern Family* and *National Lampoon's Christmas Vacation,* respectively, as characters with whom I have much in common. But I've recently begun to reconsider, based on the running gags in each character's comedy, both involving staircases.

Across his show's 11 seasons, anytime Phil trots up the stairs in a hurry, the spring in his step comes decidedly unsprung when he lands on a dislodged board and yells out on impact, "Gotta fix that step!" Clark Griswold's running gag, involving a loose newel post in his family's home, is a little subtler. But since *Christmas Vacation* is a movie rather than an open-ended sitcom, audiences do get some closure: in a bout of holiday-inspired fury, Clark, dressed in a Santa suit, uses a chainsaw to knock off the newel post entirely.

I don't have a staircase in my modest Florentine one-bedroom. But I indeed have a running gag in my renting life, and you probably do, too.

There's not been a time in the nearly-three years I've been in my home that the toilet seat wasn't a little loose or otherwise compromised.

It was a minor, pea-under-twenty-mattresses kind of issue, until it wasn't: one day recently (well, six months ago), the seat came completely dislodged, and now sits precariously balanced atop the bowl. Guests are always given due warning, and it's become like a trademarked quirk when people come over. Why rely on a signature cocktail or *antipasto* as a hostess when your theme-park-like Tuscan toilet adventure is inevitably more memorable?

Of course, it's 2020, resolution season, and way past time to get it fixed. Some people look at me slack-jawed and ask the obvious: "Why wouldn't you just call the owner?" But, without putting too much in writing, that one call would turn into... quite a lot of phone calls. Suffice it to say it'd be much easier to reach the end goal with a simple trip to a *ferramenta* or big-box supply store. (When I *did* try that, though, I was reminded of how Sam Hilt, in a 2015 article for *The Florentine,* compared Italy's vast spectrum of toilet seats to what Charles de Gaulle once said of France: 'How would you propose to govern a nation with 246 varieties of cheeses'?)

There must be more than a few of us out there who, however steadfast we may feel in our Italian footing, however self-assured we may appear as people or as inveterate Florentine renters, nonetheless get tripped up, Phil Dunphy-style, by the most unexpected and minor annoyances, errands, chores. Who knows why? Our minds and motivations are odd places, and running gags, in life as in comedy, can be oddly comforting. All I know is I felt seen this Christmas when I watched how the (monolingual!) Griswolds tacitly acknowledged their newel post and yet put off dealing with it. Given the heightened difficulties of handiwork for those of us living the Florentine rental life, well, it's probably for the best that few have easy access to chainsaws.

Vol. 28

Couched in

I was three Negronis deep with my friend Valentina recently when the conversation took a familiar turn. You know the one: discussing the merits and drawbacks of the day-to-day in our adoptive country versus our native one, and how they play into our personal psychologies.

Particularly after a certain amount of time passes, these conversations become pat and predictable, too easily facilitating defensiveness and blanket statements. They're generally not worth having in group settings, and certainly not with people who don't Get It. Yet they're illuminating and essential when held one-on-one over several years with a friend like Val. The conclusion always boils down to some variation of "there are pros and cons to every place, life is not black and white, we are fortunate to have the richness of experience that we do and the emotional fortitude that comes with it. *Evviva!* Another round!"

I was unprepared, though, for a strange talking point Val raised at our latest installment. Initially, she was sharing her appreciation of Italians' reverence for ritual, of their acknowledgment that there is a prescribed time and place for all things. But instead of banally describing how she, say, follows "the cappuccino rules"—seriously the number one motif in the flattest, get-me-out-of-here versions of this conversation—she said, "I mean, Italians sleep in the bed if they have a bed. They'd never let themselves fall asleep on the couch and just spend the night there."

Okay. I wasn't sure where that came from, but being self-involved, I thought it might be a personal callout, even though there was no way for her to possibly know that the previous night, I'd *intentionally* slept on my couch. My "I-think-I-can-I-think-I-can" washing machine had collapsed mid-cycle with all my bed linens in it, and, needing to collapse myself, I did not deal with it immediately.

But Valentina got me thinking about my sofa and the types of sofas supplied to tenants in Tuscany. "Mine" is one of the only pieces in my partially-furnished rental that I didn't buy. It's a hulking, unattractive and uncomfortable IKEA Klippan, and the shimmery slipcover I purchased for it likely cost more than the couch itself. As it is not a pullout *divano letto,* it is useless for guests, except in how it's helped me filter them out, since my litmus test now for hosting someone is whether I'd be willing to share a bed with them. (I do have an inflatable mattress in storage, but truly, who has the time?)

I'm not sure I agree with Valentina's assessment that all couch snoozing is a cultural no-no, even though she had anecdotal examples. See, the previous tenants in my place, a lovely Florentine couple, told me that it had initially been couch-less (the tiny living area is just a converted foyer). Since they'd

*It would appear,
then, that a moneyed
Florentine lady of a
certain age assumed this
couch would be suitable
for sleeping.*

wanted to have houseguests—and, you know, a place to sit—they'd asked the owner to purchase a pullout sofa, and she kindly obliged, but with a bargain-bin solution without any built-in bed.

It would appear, then, that a moneyed Florentine lady of a certain age assumed this couch would be suitable for sleeping. It'd be interesting to invite her over to try it out, but maybe not until after I move. There are times and places for things.

Vol. 29

Balance

"I'm going to have to zoom in on your face and on the food, Mary," said my cameraman colleague during a recent filming session in my kitchen. We were shooting a low-budget video about low-budget pantry staples geared at Gen-Z students in Florence.

"It's just that you don't have very pretty cabinets, so a wide shot won't look all that nice."

I raised an eyebrow and *almost* reacted defensively. But the implicit confirmation that both my canned *fagioli* and my face were prettier than the rest of the kitchen was a net positive, so I let the comment slide. No small feat! Biting my tongue on matters related to my home, its rented nature notwithstanding, doesn't come naturally to me. (Biting my tongue on basically everything else is hard, too, but I digress).

Healthy or not, I tend to look at all the aesthetic elements of my everyday life—my apartment being a prominent one—as extensions and expressions of my rawest self, which means comments about them feel personal. And since renting inevitably involves design compromises, like windowless living rooms and lowest-common-denominator cabinets, my interior decorator deep down is always bursting to tell visitors; *you know I didn't pick that out, right?* Seeking validation in this way is probably not the path to inner balance, but it does make for lively discussions.

My colleague, as it turned out, must have noticed my arched eyebrow, or else had learned a thing or two from being married: "*Non ti preoccupare,*" he rushed to add. "I know it's not *your* fault the landlord didn't provide you with pretty cabinets."

I'm not proud of how much I perked up after he said that, but I did. I may not have total inner balance, but at least I have a well-stocked pantry, which is its own kind of bliss. And I store my spices in charming glass jars with pink labels affixed to them, because you do what you can in a rental.

Vol. 30

Beat

I'm betting you landed in Florence from Far Far Away, then doggedly toiled to stay here, despite repeated admonitions to *turn back around*. Perhaps you were even in the midst of that toiling when the pandemic hit. *Si?*

It's likely, then, that your more buttoned-up loved ones use stock phrases like "she just dances to the beat of her own drum" when discussing your many charms and shortcomings. But what if I countered that you don't actually dance to the beat of your own drum? That technically, you don't dance to any "beat" at all?

You dance to the rhythm. That was my music teacher Mr. Hood's refrain back in pre-junior-high in Mississippi. "Bay-eat is what kay-eeps the mu-sic tah-geh-ther!" he'd crow insistently, clapping along to a ticking metronome to demonstrate. "See, you cain't day-ance to the bay-eat!"

Some 12-year-old walking hormone would inevitably respond to this with hammy Macarena choreography, sending his fellow hormones into raging laughter and landing in detention. The next day, Mr. Hood would switch on *The Music Man* (or *The Sandlot,* if he'd totally given up, usually around May). He'd lean back in his swivel chair, pop a Xanax (in all likelihood), and tell us we'd better keep quiet 'cause we were going to be tested on this later. All parents in Italy are Mr. Hood right now, by the way.

I committed the beat/rhythm distinction to memory, somehow. It's been a helpful lens for a Covid-19 lockdown spent alone in my Floren-tiny apartment, one marked by mostly shapeless days. *The bay-eat is what stays the same,* Mr. Hood would remind us. So I know it's Monday when I hear the masked condo cleaner mopping the stairwell. I figure it's a little after 6pm when the WhatsApps about Conte's latest press conference start trickling in. I remember I'm a living, loving, grateful-ass animal when the taste of Moka coffee makes my cells dance each (mid)-morning, or when I get the urge to write someone who hurt my feelings and ask how he's doing, or when I Google things like "banana bread easy" and "manic depression or normal pandemic anxiety?" in the span of ten minutes. Tick, tick, tick, like the metronome, day after day.

It's not so bad. But where the *bay-eat stays the same,* the *rhythm changes.* What I've missed these months is rhythm—Florentine life's little Charlie Watts-like drum flourishes (my friend calls to say she's in San Frediano, and do I want to grab a Spritz?); symphonic cymbal crashes (my landlady makes a surprise house call, and God, does my dog have to bark this much?); or sudden spits of Sean Paul verses (this one's actually just literal. My upstairs neighbors blast him at odd hours in "normal" times).

Beat is what keeps the music, and the quarantined mind, together. Zoom chats, morning coffees, and balcony singalongs have made steady-tick-tick underpinnings for our touch-hungry bodies, bruised hearts, and spiraling brains. But you can't dance to them, and I'm beyond ready for the rhythm to come back. For now, I'll have to ring in Phase 2 with a viewing of *The Music Man.*